Seasons

by Henry Pluckrose

Gareth Stevens Publishing
A WORLD ALMANAC EDUCATION GROUP COMPANY

Please visit our web site at: **www.garethstevens.com**
For a free color catalog describing Gareth Stevens' list of high-quality books
and multimedia programs, call 1-800-542-2595 (USA) or 1-800-461-9120 (Canada).
Gareth Stevens Publishing's Fax: (414) 332-3567.

Library of Congress Cataloging-in-Publication Data

Pluckrose, Henry Arthur.
    Seasons / by Henry Pluckrose. — North American ed.
        p. cm. — (Let's explore)
    Includes bibliographical references and index.
    ISBN 0-8368-2965-4 (lib. bdg.)
    1. Seasons—Juvenile literature. [1. Seasons.] I. Title.
    QB637.4.P58   2001
    508.2—dc21   2001031118

This North American edition first published in 2001 by
Gareth Stevens Publishing
A World Almanac Education Group Company
330 West Olive Street, Suite 100
Milwaukee, WI 53212 USA

This U.S. edition © 2001 by Gareth Stevens, Inc. Original edition © 2000 by Franklin Watts.
First published as *Changing Seasons* in the series *Let's Explore* in 2000 by Franklin Watts,
96 Leonard Street, London, EC2A 4XD, United Kingdom. Additional end matter © 2001
by Gareth Stevens, Inc.

Series editor: Louise John
Series designer: Jason Anscomb
Gareth Stevens editor: Monica Rausch
Gareth Stevens designer: Katherine A. Kroll

Picture credits: Steve Shott Photography cover; Ray Moller Photography title page,
pp. 9, 19; Robert Harding p. 4 (Adam Woofit), 6 (Cathy Collins), 27 (Jacobs), 31
(Robert Estall); Oxford Scientific Films p. 10 (Owen Newman); Eye Ubiquitous pp. 12
(P. Claydon), 17 (E. L. Neil); Bruce Coleman pp. 14/15 (Dr. Eckart Pott), 23 (Andrew
Purcell), 24 (Jane Burton), 28 (Bruce Coleman); Image Bank p. 20 (Pete Turner).

With thanks to: Victoria Harris.

Printed in the United States of America

1 2 3 4 5 6 7 8 9 05 04 03 02 01

Contents

Rain, sleet, wind, and snow —
winter weather is chilly! Short, cold
days follow long, frosty nights during
the season of winter.

In winter, the Sun rises low in the sky. Grass does not grow, and many trees do not have leaves. Sometimes the water in lakes and rivers freezes, or turns into ice.

Winter is the coldest season of the year. When the weather is cold, you can wear hats and mittens to stay warm. What else can you wear to stay warm?

9

Some animals grow thick coats of fur to stay warm in winter. Other animals find a place to curl up and sleep. These animals hibernate, or sleep all winter. They wake up only when the weather becomes warmer.

When the weather is warmer, winter is usually over, and the spring season begins. The Sun rises higher in the sky, and days become longer. Trees and plants start to grow leaves, and flowers, such as these daffodils, burst into bloom.

Hibernating animals wake up from their long winter sleep. Birds fly back from warm places where they spent the winter. In spring, birds build nests and lay their eggs.

When the weather becomes even warmer, summer begins. Summer is the hottest season, so we wear thin clothes to keep us cool. What else do we wear in summer?

17

In summer, we can spend lots of time outdoors. Summer is a good season for camping, fishing, or swimming. What do you like to do in summer?

Summer is also a season of big thunderstorms. On a hot summer day, dark storm clouds can bring rain. Rain makes the air feel fresh and helps plants grow.

When summer weather starts to cool, autumn, or fall, begins. During the fall season, crops that grew all summer are ready to be harvested or picked. This farmer is harvesting wheat.

Some animals are harvesting, too! This squirrel is collecting nuts. It stores the nuts so it will have food for winter, when snow covers the ground and nuts are hard to find.

In fall, the leaves on some trees change colors — from green to red, yellow, orange, or brown. After they change colors, most of these leaves drop to the ground before winter begins.

Many birds migrate, or fly to warmer places, in fall. These birds spend winter in a warm place and fly back in spring.

After fall, winter returns. Now
all four seasons — winter, spring,
summer, and fall — have passed.
A new year full of seasons begins.

Index

More Books to Read

The Fall of Freddie the Leaf. Leo F. Buscaglia (Holt Rinehart Winston)
A Little Bit of Winter. Paul Stewart (HarperTrophy)
Weather. First Discovery Book (series). Pascale De Bourgoing and Gallimar Jeunesse (Scholastic Trade)